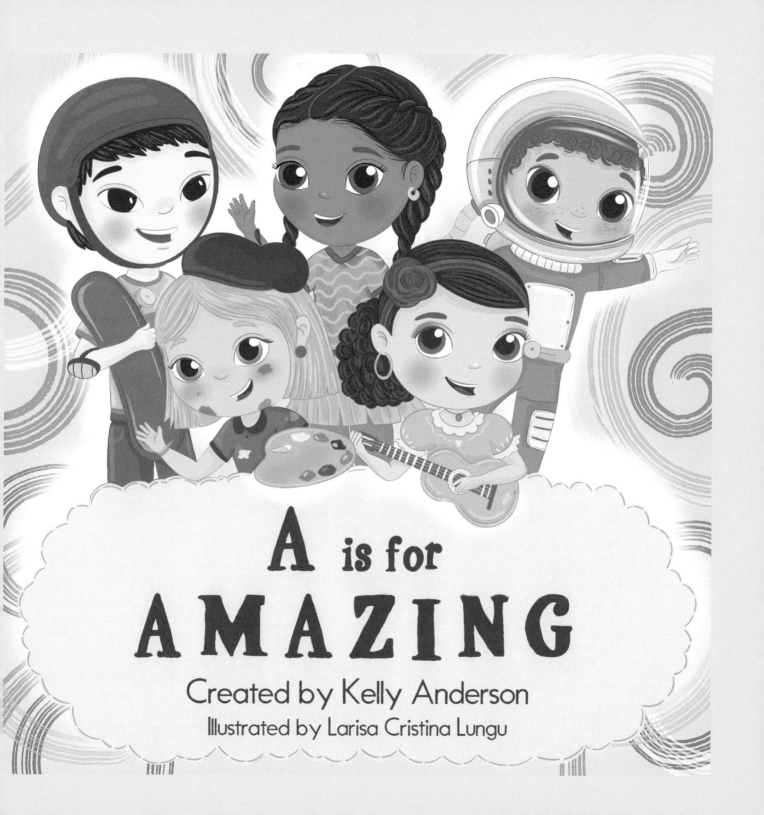

A is for
AMAZING

Created by Kelly Anderson

Illustrated by Larisa Cristina Lungu

Archway Publishing books may be ordered through booksellers or by contacting:

Archway Publishing
1663 Liberty Drive
Bloomington, IN 47403
www.archwaypublishing.com
844-669-3957

Because of the dynamic nature of the Internet, any web addresses or links contained in this book may have changed since publication and may no longer be valid. The views expressed in this work are solely those of the author and do not necessarily reflect the views of the publisher, and the publisher hereby disclaims any responsibility for them.

Any people depicted in stock imagery provided by Getty Images are models, and such images are being used for illustrative purposes only. Certain stock imagery © Getty Images.

ISBN: 978-1-6657-2620-7 (sc)
ISBN: 978-1-6657-2621-4 (hc)
ISBN: 978-1-6657-2619-1 (e)

Print information available on the last page.

Archway Publishing rev. date: 08/05/2022

Dedicated to Bianca.
All the words in this book describe you.

Acknowledgements

Many thanks to Lata, Ejiro, Elsie and Delu for their immense support and advise with the creation of this book.

This book was written and designed with love for April, Eli, Oliver, Rya, Amazing and Chimaijem in mind. I know how much joy they bring to their parents. I know *A is for Amazing* would enhance their self-confidence and provide them and every young child who reads this book with an advanced vocabulary.

Suggestions on how to read A is for Amazing

The adult should select a chosen word and say out loud to the child: For example, "You are adventurous." "You are brilliant." "You are creative." Repeat this for every word in the book.

The child should repeat after the adult: For example, "I am adventurous." "I am brilliant." I am creative", Repeat the words often until the child can say it effortlessly and use it in sentences.

Also look up the meanings of the words until the child can easily understand what each word means.

Aa
is for
Amazing **Awesome**
Authentic
Admirable
Angelic
Adorable

ADVENTUROUS

B b

is for

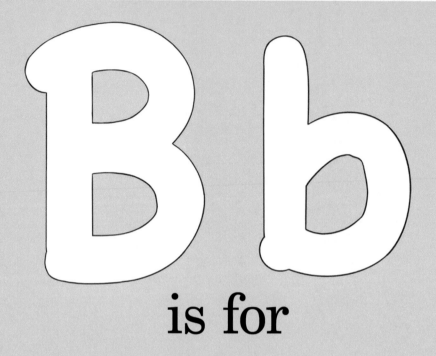

Becoming Brave

Big-hearted

Beautiful

Blessed Benevolent

BRILLIANT

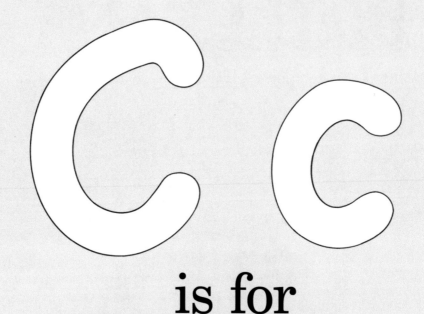

is for

Charming **Cool**

Clever Confident

Courageous

Considerate

CREATIVE

Dd

is for

Delightful Decent

Dazzling

Dependable

Dedicated

Disciplined

DYNAMIC

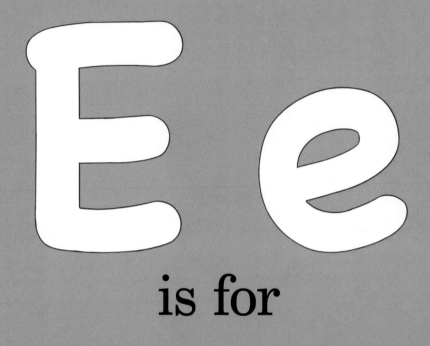

E e

is for

Exemplar

Extraordinary

Excellent Enchanting

Endearing

Enthusiastic

ELEGANT

is for

Fabulous

Friendly

Fantastic

Fascinating

Funny

Favored

FEARLESS

Gg

is for

Gusty

Genuine

Gallant

Good-natured

Genius

Gorgeous

GENEROUS

Hh

is for

Huggable

Hardworking

Heavenly

Humble

Happy-go-lucky

Handsome

HELPFUL

I i

is for

Inquisitive

Incredible

Impressive

Intelligent

Innocent

Inspiring

IMAGINATIVE

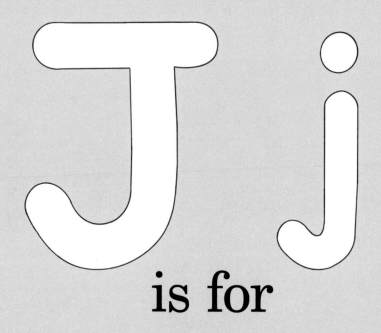

is for

Jazzy **Judicious**

Jolly

Jeweled

Jaunty

Jovial

JOYFUL

K k

is for

Kinetic Keen

Kenspeckle

Knowledgeable

Kempt **Kittenish**

KIND-HEARTED

is for

Lovely

Likable

Loyal

Lively

Legendary

Lionhearted

LIFE SAVER

Mm

is for

Marvelous

Mellow

Magnanimous

Motivated

Magnificent

Meticulous

MEGASTAR

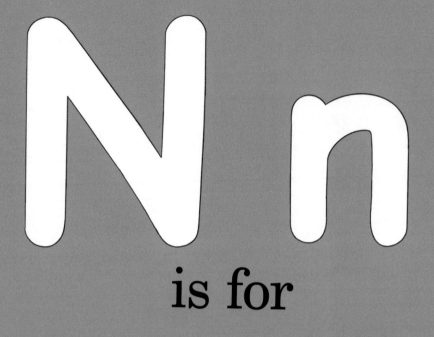

N n

is for

Natural Noble

Noteworthy

Notable

Nimble

Noticeable

NEIGHBORLY

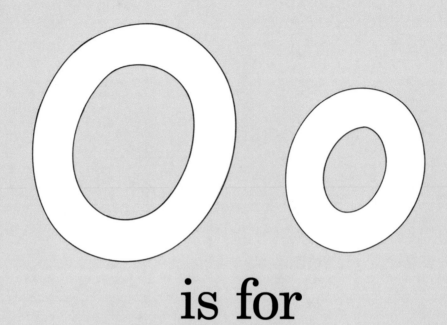

is for

Outstanding

Objective

Optimistic

Obedient

Original **Observant**

ORGANIZED

is for

Phenomenal

Perfect **Passionate**

Polite

Personable

Popular

PRICELESS

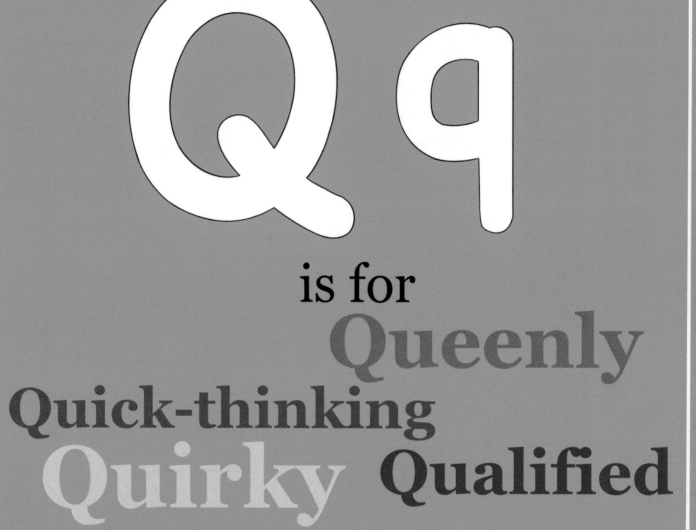

Q q

is for

Queenly

Quick-thinking

Quirky Qualified

Quick-witted

QUALIFIED

R r

is for

Respectful

Remarkable

Resilient

Radiant

Refreshing

Resourceful

RESPONSIBLE

S s

is for

Special

Superb Stunning

Sociable

Savvy Sensational

SPECTACULAR

38

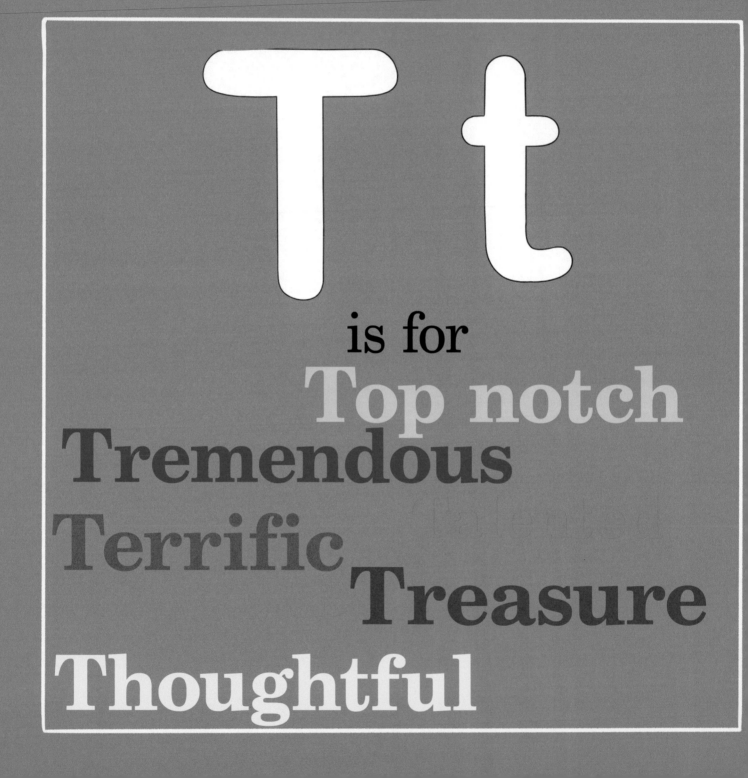

T t
is for

Top notch

Tremendous

Terrific

Treasure

Thoughtful

TEAM PLAYER

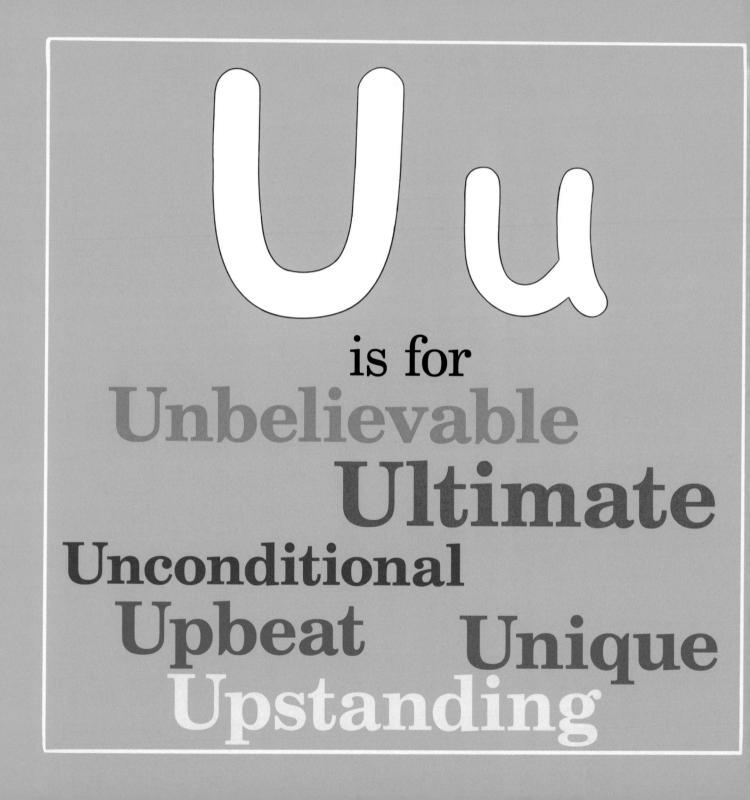

U u
is for
Unbelievable
Ultimate
Unconditional
Upbeat
Unique
Upstanding

UNSTOPPABLE

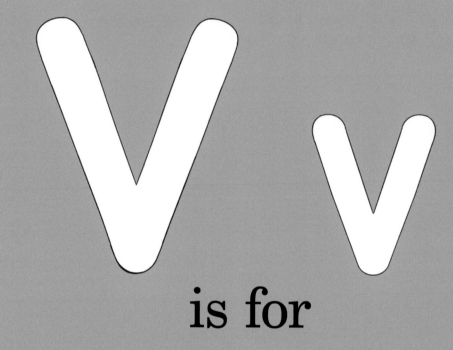

V v

is for

Valuable **Virtuous**

Vivacious

Vibrant **Valiant**

Validated

is for

Winner

Wonderful

Wholesome

Witty **Warm hearted**

Worthy

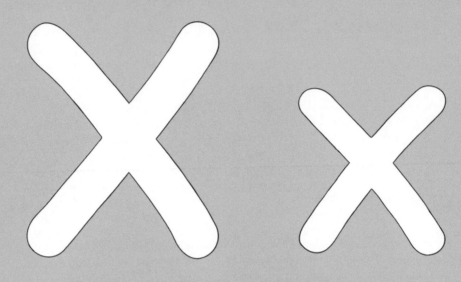

is for

Xanas

Xanolalia

Xenial **XO-XO**

Xper

Xanagogue

Y y is for

Youthful

Younker

Young looking Yern

Young at heart

Yuppie

YUMMY

Zz

is for

Zappy

Zingy

Zen

Zealous

Zazzy

Zesty

ZANY

Printed in the United States
by Baker & Taylor Publisher Services